All Dogs Are Good

POEMS & MEMORIES

COURTNEY PEPPERNELL

central
avenue
PUBLISHING

2021

Published by Central Avenue Publishing, an imprint of Central Avenue
Marketing Ltd.

centralavenuepublishing.com

ALL DOGS ARE GOOD

Trade Paper: 978-1-77168-263-3
Special Edition

Published in Canada
Printed in United States of America

1. POETRY / Subjects & Themes - Family   2. POETRY / Women Authors

10 9 8 7 6 5 4 3 2 1

For J—who loves dogs as much as I do
(well, almost).

ALSO BY COURTNEY PEPPERNELL

Pillow Thoughts
Pillow Thoughts II Healing the Heart
Pillow Thoughts III Mending the Mind
Pillow Thoughts IV Stitching the Soul
The Road Between
I Hope You Stay
Hope in the Morning
The Space Between Us
Watering the Soul
Keeping Long Island
Chasing Paper Cranes

All Dogs Are Good

PREFACE

When talking about dogs, there are three main things I think everyone can agree on. The first is that your first dog will always hold an unforgettable place in your heart; the second is that you can plan all you like for a new addition, but you almost always end up with the least expected; and the third, and perhaps the most important, is that we learn deep and invaluable life lessons from our four-legged friends.

In my early twenties, I moved into a house with a friend—the first time I had left home. While I was busy learning about all the things that meant, we were burgled. Twice. My friend, wanting some sort of security at the house, suggested we get a dog. I had always been a dog person, so I did not need to be convinced. My friend wanted a guard dog, like a German shepherd or a Doberman or a Rottweiler. I just wanted a dog. So off we went one day, my friend insisting that we were only going to look at some puppies and that nothing had been decided yet. *Yes, yes,* I remember saying, brushing him off. I was just excited to spend the day surrounded by puppies.

We arrived at the farm and greeted the owner, who led us to her barn, where the puppies were playing. The moment we walked in, eight balls of fluff went into hyper mode, each of them eager to greet the strangers. There was running and bounding and lots of excited puppy barking. My friend started a conversation with the owner, asking lots of questions about German shepherds as a breed. Meanwhile, I sat down and began to play with seven definitions of cuteness. However, it was the eighth puppy, the smallest of the pack, that caught my attention. Unlike his brothers and sisters, this particular puppy waited.

Instead of jumping all over me, he took his time before taking his moment, when the others were distracted, to sit down in front of me and stare right up into my eyes. You can imagine how I felt as I stared back down into those big brown eyes: there was not a single reason on earth that I would walk away from this dog. This dog, after all, had just picked me. So, I announced to my friend, "I'm not leaving without him," and promptly spent the last remaining funds I had in my bank account on adopting him.

In the car on the way home, we picked the name Hero, but he went on to become more than that. Hero was and still is special, because Hero was *my* first dog. We learned much about life together during this time, we moved at least four times in three years, and we used to walk miles and miles together. On these walks, I used to deliberate on the various challenges I was experiencing in my life, and Hero, I am sure, listened. We went on to navigate these life things together—like the time he rescued a baby bird, the various road trips we took, the hours I spent teaching him how to swim in the ocean, the way he would calm me down before every job interview and in the months following a breakup that nearly destroyed me. At some of my lowest points, Hero taught me what it meant to find light in our darkest hours. And for this, I cannot ever thank him enough.

Many years on, Hero and I still pacing ourselves through life, I met my wife. She was the only woman I had ever brought home that Hero didn't obnoxiously bark at. (He did turn out to be a rather good security dog.) When your dog likes them, keep them. Around two years into our relationship, she expressed wanting another dog, hinting that she wanted *her* first dog. Excitedly I rattled off some breeds: German shepherd, Saint Bernard, golden retriever, pit bull, Great Dane, border collie—but my wife shook her head and said, "I would like a Pomeranian." A Pomeranian. She wanted a Pomeranian. Well, we argued over this.

"German shepherds," I would say every night at the dinner table, "they're the best dogs. We should definitely get another one."

"You've never had a Pomeranian," she would reply. (And isn't it annoying when partners are right?)

Browsing through adoption notices one day, I came across a particular ad for the adoption of Pomeranian puppies. A young woman had taken two puppies off her parents, an accidental mishap from their dogs; however, she lived in an apartment, and her landlord discovered the puppies and told her either they went or she went. So, feeling a little sorry for this young woman and for the puppies, I suggested to my wife one evening that we go and have a look. *Just looking*, I remember saying at least seven times in the car. I think you can probably guess what happened next. When we arrived at this apartment complex, it was around 9 p.m. and dark. I am not certain my wife could even see the tiny little ball of fluff in the young woman's arms as she stood on the curbside. But even so, as we pulled up in the car and my wife opened the door, she announced, "That's *my* dog."

My friend, having come along for the ride with us, turned to me with a grin from one ear to the other. "Sound familiar?" he asked.

Obviously, we brought that puppy home. My wife named her Dakota, and it soon became clear she didn't really look like a purebred Pomeranian, leading us to believe she was mixed with something, although over the course of the next three years we've never managed to find out what. But that doesn't really matter. What matters is that I love that little dog, more than I can even put into words some days. She is what it means to find joy and laughter and light in even the littlest of things.

The most important things I've learned from my dogs are actually rather simple. They have taught me to live in every moment and follow my heart (and my nose) to the things that bring me happiness. I appreciate little things more than I did before having a dog, like sitting on the balcony in the early morning sun, slowly drinking a cup of coffee; or the first sign of fall, how the weather turns a little cooler and the leaves change, bright and colorful; or a Sunday-afternoon nap, stretched out, toes facing the fading afternoon light, daydreaming about supper. Now, as I watch them get older, I try not to think about a life without them around, and instead I think about the life that I have with them now, how lucky it makes me to know and to love two beings in this world who unconditionally and wholeheartedly choose to love me.

I dedicate this book not only to my dogs, Hero and Dakota, but also to all of yours. I hope that you find the same joy through reading these pages that I found while writing them.

PAWPRINTS

It is dawn, and so it is time to rise
to start a day filled with adventure,
perhaps leave you a little surprise.

And while you have slept,
a weathered eye on you I have kept.

For it is my duty to remind you
from dawn to dusk each day
that by your side, I shall stay.

For now, I am only a puppy,
and some days my paws feel too big.
There are so many things to play with
and so many holes to dig.

There is a whole new world to learn—
no biting, scratching, or eating the maidenhair fern,
no chewing on shoes or toilet rolls, or stealing socks,
and no surprises on the rug while you're at the shops.

And so, on my first night in this new home,
I look up and stare out at the moon,
bright and full just outside the window.
You are sleeping soundly, snoring into your pillow.

And even if there is this warm, fluffy bed—
picked out especially by you, just for me—
being in your arms is the best place to be.
Curling up next to you makes everything better,
knowing we get to be best friends forever.

It began in the middle of a storm.
I was lost, and then suddenly,
unexpectedly, I wasn't.

You found me quivering by the
storm drain. The thunder had been
too loud for my ears, and the rain,
too cold for my little bones.
You scooped me up and took me
back to the car, told your wife,
"Look what I've found."

We sat awhile, and you both
studied my tiny paws, marvelled
at how a little something like me
could exist in the world.
The scarf you were wearing looked
wonderfully warm, so this is where
I buried my nose.

Now, we lie on the sofa, often
in front of the fire, warm
and all together.
A new beginning, with years ahead
and all the sweetness to be lived.

Each time I close my eyes to sleep,
I dream of eating crumbs beneath your seat.
Of endless fields and chasing sheep
and of the many snacks you let me eat.

Of our lazy days lying in the sun
watching clouds beneath a sky of blue.
Of all our trips to the park filled with fun
and all the sticks I could possibly chew.

Of meeting new friends and lots of play
and many belly rubs all through the day.
Of all the adventures and things to do,
but mostly my dreams are filled with you.

You have many words in your world, you see
and I have very few. Here are some of my favorites:
peanut butter, swimming, walk, I love you.
And here are some of my least favorites:
bath time, hair dryer, thunder, work.

It can be confusing, all the words, you see.
Sometimes there are words you use and she does not—
You say *stay*
       and she says *wait.*
You say *on your bed*
       and she says *on your mat.*
You say *okay*
       and she says *free.*
You say *drop it*
       and she says *let go.*

But I suppose we can at least all agree on one,
each time the neighbor cat returns and I say *run*
       and you both say *no!*

Know that I hear you
each time you say you love me.
That I take it to heart when you whisper
we'll be friends forever.
Know that our meeting was no mistake.
Know that I love you a little more
with every piece of bacon that
falls from your plate.

There is nothing
like the smell of fresh air
on a beautiful summer's day,
when you and I are walking
side by side along the path
with no responsibilities in the way.
I love every walk
and every game of ball.
My heart grows more and more
every time my name is called.
Oh, how I will take these memories
through to every new life,
even the time I knocked over
the trash can and caused a little strife!

OLD HARRY

I watched you grow from reading books
and playing with toy cars.
We went on adventures through jungles
and chased UFOs all the way to Mars.

I waited for you each night,
and when it was time for bed
we'd climb the long stairs.
You'd kiss all your other animals good-night:
the blue duck, the rabbit, and the teddy bears.

And when lights were out, you'd whisper through the dark,
"Mom is asleep. Hop on the bed, Harry, but try not to bark!"

As you got older, I did too,
and when you went to college,
I promised I'd wait for you.

Now every holiday you come home,
I get so excited when you push your face
into mine and say,
"Harry, have you been a good old boy?
I brought you a new toy!"

You'll always be my best friend and I'll be yours,
you with two hands and me with four paws.

PURPOSE

It was a mystery,
why you came
to the shelter that day.
Maybe you were looking
for something.
A purpose, a dream, a wish
or a reason to stay.

But there you were,
greeting all the others
before finally stopping
to look in at me.

And I wasn't much
to look at, with bite-bitten ears
and seven missing teeth,
but I was so happy to see you
my tail wagged a little extra.

If only we could get to know
each other a little better, and
you wouldn't be just one more
to walk out the door.

So, I am sorry if I seemed
a little excited
when you pulled out
a leash.
And I covered your hands
in kisses
the moment I was released.

I was just so happy
to have found a good home,
even after all these long years
of being alone.

For a home is a home
wherever you land
and so, as fate would grant,
it was our hearts that landed
in each other's plans.

DREAMER

If you were a little more like me,
you would wake up with a smile
and roll over with little effort,
stare out the window for a while.

You would stop to greet each person
with excitement and a lot of meaning.
The more tail-wagging and sniffing the better,
for every person deserves a warm greeting.

You would notice how fresh the grass
looks, especially when newly mowed,
how every little blade is perfect
for rolling and bounding through,
such a joyous and freeing thing to do.

If you were a little more like me,
you'd smother your toast in butter
and order an extra helping of pie,
for a full belly and a long nap
are what make the world go by.

You would run the length of the pier
and dive into the open, salty sea.

And you would laugh and splash around—
completely unafraid to tell the world:
this is unapologetic me.

If you were a little more like me,
you would spend more time with
the ones you truly love.
Because true warmth and joy
lie with those we call our own
(and our own means to never ever be alone).

If you were a little more like me,
most days you would surely see—
the sun always shines a little brighter,
the daisies always smell a little sweeter,
and life is infinitely more beautiful
when you're just you: a dreamer.

THE WIDOWER

When I first came to be,
your wife knew right away
she would love me.
"Oh, this tiny thing," she said one day,
"how could we return home without her?"
"Let's go," you replied, surrendering,
and I followed you from that day forward.

And when your wife passed,
you seemed lost for a while
and there was nothing in the world
that could make you smile.
So, I made sure to bring my leash
to you whenever the sun did shine.
Our favorite thing to do was to walk,
and walk, and walk.

And one day, when the weather
was warmer, we came by a pond
with the water swelling at the sides
and fish swimming through the weeds.
Those fish, they seemed quite tricky to me.

So, I jumped into the pond,
after the fish, you see,
and oh, how you laughed.
And laughed and laughed—
the first time in forever.

Now we go to the pond at least once a day,
we watch the fish and all the people
as they pass our way, and every so often
you'll scratch me behind the ears
and with a twinkle in your eye, you'll whisper,
"Life is so much better when we're together."

There are many adventures
worth celebrating—
like rolling in the mud
and a long back-scratch.
Like a fencepost to sniff
and a Frisbee to catch.

Like running along the beach
and darting between the waves.
Like sneaking under the covers
to be closer to you when it rains.

Like leftovers snuck under the table
and fresh spring flowers in April.
Like running through sprinklers
and catching water from the hose.

But nothing beats the funny
sound you make
every time I lick your nose.

When I am with you,
there is never a better day.
But even when we can't be together
because of travel or work or play,
know that you are in my heart,
and in my heart is where you'll stay.

Where you are
should be filled
with the things
you love
and the ones
you want to see.

I suppose that's why
I am always putting
my nose in your face.

You are the most
important thing to me.

I feel joy each time I see you,
      the same joy
you seem to feel every time
you smell the poppies in our front yard.

I know that I may be a simple soul,
always watching the clouds go by
and falling asleep at the water bowl.
But it is your love and your smile
that keep my little soul whole.

The world is filled with all this wonder
      and yet it is you,
like my favorite color,
that paints my days with a brightness
      like no other.

Oh how to explain the feeling
when we are on the highway
going ninety miles per hour,
my head out the window,
ears flapping in the wind,
tongue trailing behind—
a car-surfing mastermind.

Passersby point and laugh,
waving as we go flying by.
There surely is nothing
in this world greater than
the wide open road and sky.

While waiting at traffic lights,
I see a reflection in the mirror;
could it be another car surfer,
suddenly overtaking me?
Yap yap yap—
I will not let you through!
With a shake of your head
and a hearty laugh too,
you explain, "That's you, Lou!"

DOG LOGIC

There was a day
she found me hiding in the back garden.
I was hiding because I chewed
the side of the couch.
She would be very mad
and she would say, "Bad dog! Bad!"
Only this particular day,
she crawled all the way into the shrubs,
this look of relief upon her face.
And she threw her arms around me
and said, "I found you, I found you!
Oh, what would I do without you?"
So perhaps tomorrow
I will chew the second couch.

YOU'VE GOT MAIL

There is much confusion as to why you are always mad
each and every morning, filled with such suspense
as I bark at the man with his head bobbing near our fence.

He brings you letters from far away
that smell like all sorts of things from other towns,
and all they do is make your face scrunch up,
eyebrows up into your hair, smile upside down.

So, when he comes to the gate, *BARK! BARK! BARK!*
And of course, he runs away, dropping all his papers
in a rush to get miles and miles away.

Then you run to pick them up and hurry to shut the door,
saying, "Oh, Charlie! You can't do that anymore!"

I think you must be confused as you go about your day,
because who else is going to scare that mailman away?

TWELVE MONTHS

In the first month,
I spent the nights staring at the door,
wondering why they didn't want me anymore.
Had my bow not been enough, did they tire
too quickly of my attitude?
Were they mad because of all the toys
and boots I chewed?

In the second and third months,
I watched as other dogs came and went,
wondering what they had that I didn't.
Would I ever find another home
or would I be here forever?
What did it make me
if I had no human to love,
to always be together?

In the fourth, fifth, and sixth months,
I had a roommate called Elvis, and
the ladies at the desk used to stop by
our kennel singing songs and tunes,
and for a little while I thought perhaps
all would be just fine, because I still had toys
and long, long walks in the afternoons.

In the seventh, eighth, and ninth months,
I chose to sleep a lot and didn't always feel
like eating. I still enjoyed a happy smile from
a stranger or two, but a smile from someone
who could take me home—I was still waiting
for that one, hoping it would come soon.

In the tenth and eleventh months,
a nice man from out of state knelt down
and looked in at me, a hint of sadness in his eyes.
"I wish I could take you too," he said. "But don't
lose hope, there is a family out there for you."
And I wondered that night, how long I would have
to wait for this family. And I dreamed that they
came to me in this glittering ray of light.

In the twelfth month,
the shelter strung decorations all around.
And they seemed so merry, filled with joy,
and I wondered if they had ever known
the feeling of being forgotten, discarded like an old toy.

And one evening, just before close, you came
through the door, sleet still in your hair
from all the snowfall outside.
You looked in at me and right away you said,
"Please, can I see this one?"

And I deliberated on how to trust you,
when twelve months ago I was brought here
and simply left—how easy it was for another
to throw me away and just let go.
How easy it was to be a holiday present
their children didn't want to know.

"Hello, sweet thing," you said softly,
your voice smooth like warm honey.
And into the kennel you crawled, to sit down
beside me. Reaching out a hand for my nose
to touch, you said, "They never did deserve you.
I already love you so much."

SWEET JUNE

The sweetness of June erupts in longer days
and the taste of watermelon in the air. We are
 always smiling.

We could live like this forever, cicadas calling
and ice cream cones splattered
 on the pavement.

Your nose buried in the pages of your
favorite book, we lie underneath the plum trees,
 red and rich and ripe.

And *Look, look, look,* I say with my eyes,
for a butterfly lands gently by my side.
 How we love the summer,
 spending all day outside.

HOLIDAY PARTY

It is the season for pine trees, decorated
with string lights and ornaments that look
good enough to chew. The annual holiday
party has begun. Of course, the table with
the feast is *inside*—this party is no fun.

I wait. Patiently. Patiently. Patiently.
And then, a glorious glimmer of hope:
the door is left open.

I run with all the valor a little dog has
and leap clean onto the table, oh look
at all the food, up into the air—
potatoes and parsnips, pudding and gravy,
cranberry sauce and pie and all things tasty.

Loud shrieks of despair holler into the night:
"Oh, please someone get that corgi!"
But it is far too late to catch me now;
I've already taken that first bite of turkey.

My outside plotting was far too superior
for all of your distraction by holiday cheer.
Perhaps you will think twice
about my elf costume next year.

FRIDAY NIGHTS

Every Friday night,
we talk about your problems.
Mostly it's about you not having
a date when all your friends do.

So, I sit patiently on the couch,
because once you pour that glass of wine,
I know the rest of the night
will be just you-and-me time.

We'll share a blanket and the pillows, too.
You'll cover your nose
when I let out a bad smell,
but it's not my fault that the pizza
you gave me didn't go down well.

Then we'll watch a movie,
and you might laugh, cry, or scream,
and I'll jump up and howl at the screen.

Friday nights are my favorites with you,
which is why, if you ever do get a date,
I'll judge them like it's the last thing I'll do.

SECRET KEEPER

You can tell me all your secrets,
like how someone broke your heart
or how you stole money from
Mom's purse.

You can tell me all your dreams,
your fears,
and questions about the universe.

You can throw the stick as far
as you want,
you can play ball with me
until the sun goes down.

You can chase me
when it's bath time,
and you can always count
on me to be around.

Last night while you slept,
I came to you in a dream
and I whispered—

That while I am no longer there,
I am still with you in our memories
and everything in between.

I rested my head next to yours
in the way I always used to do,
and I wished upon the brightest star
you'd no longer be sad and blue.

Sometimes I hear you as you weep,
because the truth doesn't seem fair;
how could it be that a lifetime for me
is a only chapter for you?
But I promise you don't have to worry—

For I am forever sleeping
under my favorite maple tree,
and someday when your path ends,
together we'll be again
for eternity,
just you and me.

A LETTER TO YOU

If you could hear me
in words that you understood,
I would say
there are many things in this life
that will weigh heavy in your
heart and mind and soul.

There are many responsibilities,
like bills and homework and chores.
And feelings of stress and anxiety
that always make you feel
a little less of a person,
a little less whole.

How to cope when these things
feel so overwhelming?
Days filled with despair
to break your heart in two.
All these doubts and fears
of what others might think of you.

But try to remember, it's the little
things in life that make us smile
the most. Like long car rides,
the sun on your face, and Sunday roast.

Like rolling in mud or sand,
the smell of late-night air,
a laugh with a friend
or a hand in your hair.

Like cozy blankets,
always so soft and warm,
and sitting out on the porch
as I roll in our freshly cut lawn.

These little things in life
that bring me joy,
I hope bring you joy, too.
For no matter how hard
a day may be,
it's the little moments
we need to hold on to.

It's the little moments
that remind us:
You have me and I have you.

THE FUN PARK (WITH ROCKY)

"Park" is a word I do so enjoy;
it gives me the same feeling in my tummy
as when you tell me I am your good boy.

Today, as I slept by the stairwell
and dreamt of warm apple pie,
you called out the magic word,
and up went my ears to the sky.

Leaping into the car, my heart racing
a million beats in a single minute—
for the park is always my
favorite place to visit.

But soon it became quite apparent
we were going on by the park today.
There I was, watching it fade away.
(Perhaps it's possible you forgot the way.)

We were *supposed* to be going
to the fun park,
at least this is what it usually means
every time you say,
"Rocky, let's go play."
Then why is there no fun park today?

I whine from the back seat, *This is the pits!*
"Oh Rocky," you reply sheepishly
from behind the wheel,
"I don't think you are going to like this."

For this is no ride to the beloved fun park, you see.
I know exactly where you are taking me.
As we pull into the big old parking lot,
it becomes apparent that I have been tricked,
for today is the day my bits get fixed!

MAY WE MEET AGAIN

I know it doesn't seem fair that I had to leave,
and you needed to collect all my old toys;
I know it will take some time for the tears to dry,
and to remember the memories
and all the moments filled with joy.

When the sun rises and a new day comes to be,
I know that old habits will make you think of me—
the worn-out stuffed rabbit, my favorite,
still out on the lawn with only one eye;
stepping back from the counter, a finger pointed,
"Max," you would say, "do not touch the pie!"

A thudding sound upstairs, could it be me,
running down the hall once more?
In the late fading sunlight,
you might even stop a moment,
thinking you saw me at the back door.

While it may seem impossible
to bring a new friend home after staring
at my empty bowl for far too long,
in time your heart will heal and open a special
space for a friend who needs
a home, a hand, and a warm place.

My greatest wish, in the moments
you are remembering my name,
is that I remain a little light forever
resting deep within your heart,
a place that was always mine,
right from the very start.

For now, when I visit you
in your dreams,
I hope you hear me whisper
that when you've lived your journey,
we'll be sure to meet again,
my dearest and truest friend.

GOLDEN HOUR

This day is the kind of day
you never forget—

We ride with the windows down,
the smell of saltwater drawing closer
with every passing tree on the coastline.

The sound of waves breaking onto the shore
as we run for the sparkling water together—
there is nothing in the world I love more.

And as golden hour touches your skin, we
walk for miles, inspecting ocean treasures
washed ashore by turquoise tides.

"Atlas," you call as I bound through whitewash foam,
your voice, always the song to call me back home.
"Let's stay awhile," you say.

So, as the sun slips from the sky, swallowed by sea,
we sit, side by side,
and we watch the surfers from afar—
I hope you always know,
my heart is wherever you are.

There is no need for pretending
when it comes to my loyalty to you.
There is no need for grand gestures or acts,
because this love of ours is a lifelong pact.

There is no need for pretending
when you feel worthless or troubled or blue,
for my only wish in life is to comfort you.

I'd walk one thousand miles to pull you
from all the rubble burying your heart,
for in the moments that you need me most,
it's my job to ensure you don't feel so lost.

With the tears streaming down your face
and the rain pouring outside, I place my paw
on your knee. Can't you see my big brown eyes
staring right into yours?

There is no need for pretending,
for all that I am and all I will ever be,
is to exist in this life
so that I can be here for you,
and you can be here for me.

We'll always be together,
connected by a thread only you and I can see.
For every time you look at the golden sun,
you'll remember the days I used to run and run.

For every time you see a shooting star,
you'll remember I will never be too far.

On the days you need to find me,
close your eyes and open your heart.

It is there we share all our sweet memories,
so, for all of time, we'll never be apart.

Now why won't you let me chase the squirrel
all the way up the tree?
It only appears in the dusk, surely just to tease me.
Darting this way and that way, how I long to run.
Please, please, please—just a little harmless fun.

And then you appear with that same old tone.
"Winnie," you say sternly, "leave that squirrel alone."

Oh, but there is the squirrel, how little is he,
snooping around for acorns underneath the tree.
I just need to tell him to search in a different place.
Surely, he should know this is my spot to pee.

Out like a flash I launch as fast as I can, hardly able
to contain my excitement—*Run, run, run.*
For a moment the squirrel looks right at me, and I think
perhaps today, we'll get the chance to be friendly.

But as I near, the squirrel takes off in a wink, his bushy tail
disappearing high up into the branches—
and as I watch, hoping for a change in circumstances,
suddenly the tree looms in front of me.
Paws won't stop, and I collide, leaves whooshing everywhere.
Upside down in the grass, legs splayed in the air.

And suddenly there you are with your hands on your hips,
a big smile upon your lips.
"Oh Winnie," you sigh, "I told you not to try!"

THE 'W' WORD

The bright sun began to stream into the room.
"Good morning," it said. "A brand-new day."
So, I stretched my paws
and crawled over to where your sleeping head lay.
Wake up! I'm ready for that favorite word you always say.

Up and out of bed you got, messy hair and a yawn,
brushing your teeth to a tune and clumsily finding your pants.
Let's go, let's go, this is all going much too slow.
You're not much of a morning person, I will admit.

Out came the socks. *Quickly! I am about to lose it!*
And then the shoes, the special kind for outdoors.
One shoelace, two shoelaces, all tied up,
and we were bounding to the floor.

Finding the collar and leash (I could barely contain myself).
Hey, don't forget those little bags on top of the shelf.

You looked down at me and asked with a smile,
"Are you ready?"
Yes, can't you see all the excitement bubbling inside of me?
For you were about to say my favorite sound to be heard—
oh, how happy it makes me every single morning—
this glorious, wonderful, magical 'W' word:

"W A L K I E S!"

SPARROW IN THE SNOW

It was early November when the snow began to fall
in pockets all around the neighborhood.
Frosty car windows and rooftops all around,
snow piles and icicles all over town.

One day, when the sun shone, we decided to go
for a long walk along our usual trail,
the hidden path where no one goes.
So off we went into the woods,
one snowflake, two snowflakes, kissing my nose.

All around the trail, white powder continued to fall,
and we left no leaf unturned, no buried flower unseen,
inspecting every fallen branch of every evergreen.

In the powdery frost, I discovered a lost scarf,
distracted only for a moment before hearing your
voice in the distance.
"Sparrow," you called, and I bounded over to you,
following you along the path.

And as I looked back at my pawprints, right next to yours,
I realized that life was meant to be walked
side by side with you, this love
the greatest thing I will ever know,
a story of two souls walking through the woods
with our footprints and pawprints written in the snow.

LATE JULY

This is my favorite season, when the days
stretch long into the night,
the sky the color of jeans and blueberries,
the moon hanging beautiful and delicate,
waiting for the endless canvas to turn to velvet.

We run wild and free along the sand,
the golden light of the sun—such delight.
The glow of the waves meeting the shoreline,
all those seashells, stories from the ocean.
The wind in my curly hair, my family chases me,
kicking up sand, laughing and calling out,
"Catch the ball, Oscar, hurry!"

The half-bald tennis ball between my teeth,
the salty sea beneath my paws, the surf churning.
Racing after every throw, darting through the foam,
the horizon calling the fading light back home.
Bundled in arms that hold me close to the heart,
a soft kiss upon my head, a promise we'll never part.

The air still perfectly warm as we lie content
and tired from all the running and the play,
but there is no other wondrous feeling
quite like a late July day. We have

time.

FOOTPRINTS

May you go through life
with one foot in front of the other.

May you find joy and adventure
and dream beautiful dreams
all through the night.

May you be accompanied
by a four-legged friend
to fill your days with light.

Through the off-beaten track my shepherd
    leads,
each pawprint left behind in the dirt path
a memory to hold on to
    forever.
At the edge of the forest, the birds sing in the trees,
    a melody for a beautiful day.

And emerging from the leafy canopy,
    a small, long-winged songbird takes flight.
We watch together the beauty of the swallow,

    for wherever my shepherd walks in this sleepy little life,
I, too, shall follow.

I once met a man
and he did not have a home,
but he said to me,
"Child, you misunderstand,
for I have a dog,
and with my dog
I am never alone."

Rolling onto his back
with legs high in the air,
a toothy grin
and standard bed hair,
my dog says,
Good morning.
What are we having for breakfast?

On a day where you spill your coffee
and get stuck in traffic,
when there's too much work
and your boss is far too bossy,
you'll come home
and there will be a happy face waiting,
with ears that have heard you coming
and an excited tail wagging.

My dog teaches me to live every day with love.
A sad moment can be fixed with a hug and a
face that knows, and following your heart is
as good as following your nose.

My dog teaches me that afternoon walks
are perfect for the soul, that naps by the fire
are as important as eating sandwiches whole.

My dog teaches me that selflessness is needed,
friendship takes you far, and loyalty should
exist in every season, no matter who you are.

When you were a puppy,
your tummy used to bloat
after every meal.

You slept right next to my face
and chewed my hair in the
middle of the night.
You stood up to strangers,
barking with all that tiny might.

We used to run around in the yard
until you fell asleep right in the
middle of the grass, and I would
pick you up in my arms and
take you back inside.

In summer when it was time to play,
there was no place you couldn't
seek to my hide.

As you got older, you became bigger
than me, and I knew you would
protect me from all the things
I could or couldn't see.

There have been many moments in my life
where I have been caught by surprise:
the time all my laundry turned pink or the day
I had no umbrella and rain poured from the sky.
But I must admit the moment I did not see
was when I was taking a bubble bath and, thinking
I needed rescuing, my dog jumped in after me.

LUNA, NAMED AFTER THE MOON

THIS IS THE STORY OF A YOUNG WOMAN FROM MAINE AND her dog Luna, salt-and-pepper in color, named after the moon. Of how Luna arrived at a time the young woman needed solace,

when the world felt too unforgiving

and dark and thoughtless.

One night, by the windowsill the young woman sat, searching through the sky,

hoping for an answer to the feelings

she felt deep inside.

In these moments when she did not feel full or heard or whole,

> would there be an answer, to sew back

> > the seams that stitched her very soul?

Beside her, Luna gazed up at her dreamily, eyes filled with light, as if to say the young woman was just as beautiful as the moon in the night. And the woman asked the moon if she ever felt she was truly needed in the same way that the earth had always needed the warmth of the sun.

> If she had as much purpose in the moments

> > she felt she was coming undone.

And the moon said, while it took some time, she understood she was beautiful, even when only half, for while she was not always whole, she was always the light in the dark. In the morning when the sun rose and daylight returned, she would remember her purpose for the next night, that when the world slept and the shadows played,

> she was the guiding light,

> > bringing the stars and souls into a new day.

So, the young woman considered, while some nights were harder than others, there would always be room in her heart for many things, like leaves in the fall and seashells on the shore, like the strength and purpose that would find her soon,

> and Luna, of course,

> > named after the moon.

If, when I die,
I am greeted by all the dogs
I've ever parted with and loved,
then leaving this earth
for the next adventure
holds just a little less fear
and a little more worth.

You'll remember them forever,
especially when you grow up
and have a family of your own.

You'll share childhood memories
and laugh about the things your friends
with paws used to do.
There is reason in why they came to you.
Purpose for the lessons they taught you.

And when you are older, you'll remember
the four-legged friends who stayed true to you.

Dogs teach us the importance
of love and loss.
That each and every day
is another chapter in your story.
Despite the day being easy or
difficult or in between,
despite the day being ordinary
or extraordinary, every day matters;
there are so many reasons to be grateful.

When they are dreaming
   and their nose is twitching
   and their paws are running,
I like to imagine
   they are thinking of you.
Someplace where you are never out of reach,
somewhere you can be together for always.

One of my favorite things
is looking over at my dog
and seeing that he is always
looking at me.
And I ask him,
"What you are doing?"
like he will understand me,
and I know he won't.
But he wags his tail as if he can.

In my deepest, darkest moments,
there was my dog.
He would not leave my side.
There was no place
I could run to or hide;
he would always find me.

And I needed this.
I needed someone
to sit in silence with.

Someone who would
never judge me for the pain I felt.
Someone who would let me grieve
the things I thought I had lost.
Because I understood then
that I hadn't lost anything at all.
I was still here.
I was still living and breathing.

One day, when I pulled back the
curtains of my dark and dusty bedroom,
my dog stood in the doorway
as if to say,
I know you have been sad,
but I always knew you would come home.

LILY, BOBBY, TREVOR, ASTRO, AND KLEIN

On Tuesdays, I walk the short walk to the local café.
I order a coffee, and sometimes a bagel.
I sit at the same table in the corner, near the door.
I like to watch the people come and go,
drink my coffee, sometimes two or three or more.

On this Tuesday, a man stops outside with his little
brown dog. He sets her down and ties the leash to a chair
before he looks the little dog in the eyes and says,
"Stay here, Lily, I won't be gone long."

Into the café the man walks, his boots striding along,
and he orders his coffee and looks back at his dog.
Smiling a big smile, he says to the others in line,
"Adopted that one, can't believe she's mine!"
And the other patrons all agree and take out their phones—
"This is mine."
And so I listen to the chatter as they boast about
Bobby and Trevor and Astro and Klein.

Collecting his coffee, the man returns outside to Lily,
and she greets him with an excited tail wag
as though she hasn't seen him forever.
And now, each Tuesday I see dogs waiting by the café door,
and they all remind me of what truly matters in this world.

That a soul is a soul no matter the skin,
and a heart is a heart no matter the body it beats within.
That all walks of life can be considered a family.
Such hope this gives me, for our dear humanity.

WHAT IS A FOOTSIE?

On a cool, brisk morning in the middle of November,
I left my terrace and passed under the jacaranda trees
        with my little dog Dakota
        walking steadfast beside me.

We stopped once, twice, three times
to inspect the trunks of the trees,
the small garden patch,
and the abandoned candy wrapper.

We waved to the lady sitting outside,
a familiar face at the community centre.
So, too, the children chattering away
outside the bus stop on their way to school,
and a handyman climbing down from a ladder.

We crossed the road, looked both ways,
and drifted idly toward the smell
of our favorite coffee beans.

Outside the coffee shop (heaven's gates),
two young girls waited with their father,
and they took turns dancing around the streetlamp,
singing in the misty morning frost.

And as we approached, the taller girl pointed,
excitement flushed upon her cheeks.

"Look!" And at Dakota they both looked.
Said she to the other, "She looks like a Footsie."
"Yes," agreed the other, "a Footsie."

Said Dakota, *What is a Footsie?*

"Well, I do not know," I replied thoughtfully.
Could it be that there was another dog
in the world with this name of Footsie?

And the girls continued to point, with wide
smiles upon their faces.
"A Footsie!" they called.
"A Footsie," they sang.
Round and round the streetlamps they danced.

And as we stood in the cool morning breeze,
the sunlight warming the pavement,
the slow pull of traffic building
and the coffee grinder whirling,
I determined this could be but one thing.

So, I glanced down at Dakota to tell her so—

"A Footsie is the joy a little dog like you
brings to all sorts of people as you pass their way
and, all things considered, I think we can agree,
everyone deserves a little joy to start their day."

Your dog will never
wake up one day
and decide they no longer
want to be in your life.

They will never pack a bag
or tell you
that you aren't enough.

They'll never hurt you
or call you names.

They will never judge you
for the things you know,
or the things you don't.

The only time they will
ever break your heart
is when they have lived
and it's their time to go.

There is nothing like reading a good book
with your dog warming your feet

There is nothing like an early morning run
with your dog by your side

There is nothing like cooking dinner
with your dog at your heel

There is no better way for your day to start
than having your dog in your heart

THE NEW BARN DOG

Far from somewhere you and I would know, there is a sleepy little town, one someone might fly over on their way to somewhere else. A town left off most maps, hidden by bends in the road and whispers in the trees. But if you were to stop, the air would feel lighter and taste a little sweeter. In the late summer, between the rolling hills and highways that go on for miles, you would see the grass lacing itself together, holding hands. You would see the rows and rows of cornfields, an endless golden painting with splashes of green. If you went a little further down the road, you would stumble across an old farm, its very heart beating beneath the soil, and with every sunset, it would seem as though the sky swallowed it whole.

In between the farmhouse and a giant oak tree is the barn—big old doors, brass handles, painted red and white. In the barn is where all the animals live, like Horse and Cow and Rooster, and now Maverick, the new barn dog.

"That's the new barn dog," said Horse to Rooster, one day in the spring.

"He's a little small," replied Rooster. "How is he going to get anything done?"

"I wish the old barn dog were still here," said Cow. "At least she always knew what to do."

On his first day, Maverick walked into the barn, dewdrops glistening in his hair from an early morning run.

"Good morning," he said. "I am going to herd the sheep into the new paddock."

Rooster scoffed, "They won't follow you!"

Despite the discouragement, Maverick walked toward the sheep and told them today they would be going to the new paddock. Without even lifting their heads, the sheep bleated for him to go away.

"See," said Horse, "they will only listen to the old barn dog."

Yet Maverick continued trying to move the sheep. He moved around them and in front of them and behind them. And still, the sheep continued to go in all different directions, moving this way and moving that way, but never falling into line.

"He should just give up," said Cow. "He has lost."

Sometimes people are a little like that; they have more faith in the old ways rather than the new, but faith is also born of persistence. So Maverick persisted. He continued moving around the herd and then around the other way, again and again. Until finally, the herd began to go in the direction they were supposed to. Eventually, with the sheep tucked in their new paddock, bleating happily, Maverick returned to the barn.

Said Maverick, "I only lose if I stop trying."

And Horse and Cow and Rooster all agreed.

WARM TOES

I was so exhausted the other day,
and I was cold because all my socks
were in the laundry.
So, I was complaining as I sat at my desk,
"My toes are cold, my toes are cold."

And then you got up from where you had
been asleep on your bed and you lay across my feet.

I remember looking at you in mild wonder;
was it a coincidence or not—had you heard what I had said?

Even so, as you lay there with your soft sable coat,
my toes began to warm.

If I could do my life over, I would surely ask for a soul
just like yours. Because you are generous and loving,
you are courageous and bold.

Wouldn't it be nice to always be
the kind of soul that keeps toes warm
when they're cold?

HAPPINESS

Happiness is coming home to you
when your tail is wagging
and you're sitting on your
favorite chair.

It's jumping in the car and heading
to the beach
with the sand in your fur
and your tongue in the air.

It's waking up in the morning
and seeing you asleep
at the end of the bed.

It's staying in on the weekend
and watching a movie with you instead.

It's having you to wish
all my troubles away,
and it's knowing that in your heart,
I'll always stay.

INTO THE LAKE

We'd driven down to the lake for the weekend.
A week of rain had the hills looking greener,
the flowers glistening in dewdrop sugar.

And my dog had his head out the window,
soaking in the sunlight with our favorite
playlist on the radio.

Floating on our backs in the water, the lake
sprawled for miles, lily pads, brushing my skin
like stolen kisses, disappearing in the wind.

A day to find hope and dreams and be closer
with the earth, to forget all my worries and
battles with self-worth.

Perhaps I can pretend, if only for a minute,
my arms are wide enough to envelop
the whole wide world
and hold every soul in my heart, remind them
that despite all their doubts, they aren't alone.

And yet perhaps this is what dogs already do.

EACH DAY

Each morning is the same.
We walk by the post office,
we stop to smell the roses,
we wave to the lady
at the end of the street,
hosing down her driveway.

We pick up the pace past the school,
past the bakery. You lift your nose high
into the air—*Should we stop for a croissant?*—
like it's a dare.

You remain excited, interested,
no matter how many times
we have walked the same way.

Live each day like you are living
for the first time—at least this is what
I believe you are trying to say.

I am sure you would agree,
when a dog comes into your life
things are bound to change,
and schedules surely rearrange!

Handfuls of fur in all kinds of spaces,
and hiding treats in unimaginable places.
A tail always wagging by the door,
and toys strewn out all over the floor.

The way your heart smiles and laughs,
even on days destruction is in your path,
like an interrupted bubble bath
and a toilet-paper aftermath.

All house appliances become enemies—
the vacuum, the lawn mower, even the garden rake,
not to mention those eyes staring directly into your soul
every time someone has a birthday cake.

A LIFETIME OF LOVE

Even if they do not speak
the same language as us,
they still love when you
speak to them as though they do.

When you break their treats into
sizes just for them, when you come
home with a new toy and spend
extra time fussing over their needs.

They love the moment you walk
through the door and that you come
to them when you are sad.
They love that when they walk dirt
into the house, you still have time
for cuddles even when you're mad.

They love when you hide,
and they get excited when they find you.
They love that high-pitched
voice you do.

They love how much they are your baby
even as they get old, and those nights
watching movies by the fire when it's cold.
They love when they feel too tired and
you'll lie with them on the floor.

Most of all, they love how every day
goes past and you love them more and more.
They will come and they will go,
and you'll wonder why they couldn't
stay a lifetime.

It would be much better
if they could stay forever.

But they are here a short while
to teach us,
even if life can be difficult
and things don't always go our way,
it is important to forgive
and show kindness every day.

I have a very clear picture of you
that afternoon in the park.
I turned my back for only a moment
and then there you were,
sailing through the air,
tongue flying, paws outstretched.
Incoming hug, I thought,
would have been better
without all the mud.

I have a catalog of memories that I will keep forever. But the day we went to the beach and I taught you how to swim will always be one of my favorites. There you were, kicking up sand and trying to bite the sea, and I couldn't help but wonder how ridiculous we would have looked, just you and me. But your bark rang out into the wind, as did my laugh. I'll remember how excited you were by the waves, how we ran from them tumbling onto the shore. I'll think back to that day, and I'll cherish the moment, right down to my core.

HEARTBREAK MEDICINE

The heartbreak happened in late August.
My heart, once so full, was now empty.
I would cry almost every night
for a love I thought I knew.
Everything had surely changed,
ripped from deep within me.

Everything, except for you.
You were always with me.

Each night I would crawl into bed,
my heart feeling heavy from the ache,
wondering why I wasn't good enough
or if I would ever find love again.

The door would open wide, and I'd hear
your paws pad across the floor,
tail wagging in the air.

You would make your way to my side
of the bed and press your nose into my face.
You would watch me as I fell asleep,
and even if your soft fur tickled my cheeks,
I didn't care, because when it felt like everything
had fallen apart, you were always right there.

PUPPY GRADUATION

Awake at the first sign of dawn,
bounding through the living room.
Jump, jump, jump.
       First day of school.

The class is filled with eager little things,
their eyes growing wide at the size of you.
Run, run, run.
       All fall down like bowling pins.

"He is too big for this class," the instructor says.
You look up at me.
But it is not my fault my paws are too big.
       Why don't I fit?

We do not get the graduation certificate.
Walking back to the car, sitting in the front seat,
I pull you into my arms; *this* is a perfect fit.
       It's settled—

I'll print one off at home.

THE SAINT BERNARD FROM MY HOMETOWN

IN MY HOMETOWN, WE ONLY HAD ONE LIBRARY; IT WAS RUN like clockwork by Mrs. Brown, and some would say her Saint Bernard, Duke. Each day, Duke would sit at the entrance of the library and greet the townsfolk, and he would get all sorts of compliments and treats. Everybody in town loved Duke. Even the cat lovers loved Duke. When I was in high school, I spent much of my time in the library, reading. I could be lost for hours in new cities and worlds, grappling with stories that would carry over into my dreams.

Each time I entered the library and left the library, Duke would hold out a paw for me to shake, in what I assumed was a hello and a see-you-soon.

One such week, rather than the usual hello or goodbye, I received a rather intimidating bark, and in fact every day that week, Duke would continue to bark at me, to the point where I was beginning to feel as though Duke no longer liked me.

On Friday, midafternoon, Mrs. Brown was filling up Duke's water bowl, and like all the other days that week, Duke again barked at me.

"Mrs. Brown," I said, exasperated, "I don't think Duke likes me anymore. He has barked at me all week."

Mrs. Brown looked at Duke with interest and then back to me.

"Do you have any overdue library books?" she asked.

I shook my head, confused. "No!"

"Are you sure?"

I buried myself in my bag, and Duke became excited, wagging his tail and barking some more.

Sure enough, at the very bottom of my bag, underneath a forgotten packed lunch, a sweater, and an inkless pen, I found the library book I thought I had lost.

Mrs. Brown just smiled, opening the library return box. "We'll waive the late fee, dear," she said.

And I'll tell you one thing: in my hometown, a library book is still never overdue.

ZOOMIES

[Zoo-m-ee-s] · *plural*

Standing on the back porch, a cup of tea in hand,
        I watch
while you zoom around in the long, spindly grass
like a rocket has been strapped to your back.

How happy you look, running to this side
        and running to that side,
barely able to contain your grin,
soaring through the air, pouncing on wildflowers,
dancing around under the sky for hours and hours.

"Yes," I think, "let's stay awhile."
        There is nothing more sure to make me smile.

A DOG

Sometimes I dream about the things
I could have been.
Somewhere in the universe,
there are different versions
of who I am and who I came to be.

Perhaps I am a pilot,
without a fear of flying.
Perhaps I live along the coast
with a sailboat in the driveway,
or in a lodge way up in the mountains.
Perhaps I have had my heart broken less,
or perhaps I have fallen in love more.

I like to imagine these other versions
of me are happy, cared for, in charge
of their destiny.

But in every version of every life,
I know that I have a dog.

YUKE, THE RESCUE

There was a dog the color of midnight
lost in the woods beyond the highway,
scared and alone, having run away from home.
For in this home, she was not treated right,
always left in the cold and never told she belonged.
So, feeling hopeless, she ran away in the night.

And on this night, I found her in the rain,
a little broken, full of pain, without a smile.
So, rushing over, I put my arms around her,
told her to come inside my home for a while.

And home it became, with all the toys I bought,
the warm bed I made, and all the tricks I taught.
I gave her a new name, Yuke, meaning strength,
promised she would be safer here, with every breath.

Now, every night before she sleeps,
I remind her we are more than the things that
make us feel haunted.
That for the rest of her days, she will be loved
and forever wanted.
I tell her not to think of the past, all that was and were.
because Yuke now belongs to me, and I belong to her.

SIMPLE THINGS

While young and free-spirited,
my dog taught me many things—
that excitement could be found
in skipping stones on the river;
that there is always time to breathe,
even when life wreaks havoc;
and that sunlight peeping in between
the trees is the closest thing to magic.

And when growing old and gray,
my dog still saw the beauty in each day,
even on a day that was bleak and rainy,
even on a day our bones were a little achy.

Now I try to live each day a little better,
show more forgiveness and gratitude,
be more open to what I don't always know.
Show more excitement for the simple things,
like flower petals and the first sign of snow.

When I was younger, I struggled with the person in the mirror. I didn't think it was possible that anyone would want to love me. I didn't think I deserved it any more than the anger of a storm at sea. I wondered if life was meant for people who always seemed to be alone, I wondered if everyone had different versions of what made a home.

But then I found my dog, or rather my dog found me.

And I started to understand what it meant to love the simple things around us. Like the sun on my skin, the flowers in the garden, and the importance of letting others in.

So, the love for myself grew, opening like a bud and blooming toward the sky. Now here we are living for warm days, ball in the park, watching the cars go by. Even after all this time, I may have grown all this love for myself, I may have won an inner war, but I know without a doubt, my dog loves me more.

There will be times
in your life
where you will reach
for a hand
and get a paw instead.

WHEN FOREVER BEGAN

We brought you home
a little before dinnertime,
with your weary eyes
and fading gray snout.

They told us to leave the light on
because you were afraid of the dark.

And I wanted to ask why,
but the look on your face
told me you'd had enough.
That all you truly wanted was
someplace warm, somewhere
you could lie down and rest.

But there had been a storm that day
and all the power was out.
I knew when we got you inside
you were already afraid.
So, I took you in my arms,
held you close to my chest,
whispered things like
"You're safe, you will only get the best."

I knew you had been mistreated;
promises made had been broken before,
so how could you think we would be
any different the moment we brought
you through our door?

So, I lit some candles and
settled into the couch.
I wrapped you tighter in my arms
and promised I'd stay with you.

When I opened my eyes again
the power must have come back on,
but the morning sun
was coming through our window,
pouring in the light.

And I looked at you,
still safely in my arms,
and you looked back at me, happier
because I'd kept my promise—

I'd stayed with you through the night.

Tomorrow when I wake,
there will no longer be your
furry head sharing my pillow.

In the morning, sipping my coffee,
staring out at the willow in the yard,
there will no longer be a tail wagging,
eyes staring up at me.

As a siren wails on past the house,
there will no longer be a howl
of a melody in return.

When the doorbell rings, there will be
no one racing to greet the person
on the other side, tail in the air,
barking as loudly as one thinks fair.

And the hole in my heart feels greater
than a hole should be. And sometimes
as I stare out onto the porch,
imagining you sleeping in the sun,
I catch a glimpse of you in the light,
and it gives me hope
that I will see you in my dreams tonight.

A dog's purpose is to find
the deepest part of your heart,
in which they will stay,
just for the thought
of walking beside you
one more day.

HERO, TEACHING DAKOTA

One evening when the moon was full,
Hero said to Dakota, "I am to teach you a lesson."
Dakota replied, "Could we do this after supper? I am
hoping to catch some crumbs falling to the floor."
Hero stood up, shaking his head.
"This, my friend, is an important lesson."

So over to my wife he went, and he barked once.

"One minute," she replied. "I'll feed you then."

Stretching wide, paws out in front, he barked again,
big brown eyes staring longingly into hers.
So, my wife paused preparing our supper and piled
deliciousness into Hero's bowl.

He ate happily.

Sitting back down, Dakota asked,
"Well, what was the lesson?"

Just then I walked down the stairs, and my wife said, "I fed Hero."

"Oh," I replied, "I already fed him an hour ago."

And Hero smiled.

LIFE ACCORDING TO TEDDY

If Teddy, a bulldog with ears as soft as butter
and a smile so big it makes your heart flutter,
wrote you a letter—this is what it would say:

I hope you laugh, long and from the belly,
let the sound fill the air so that others will hear.
I hope you sing songs as loud as you can, hold
the people you love a little longer, a little nearer.
I hope you understand the greatest
acts of love are often silent, like lying on the
floor next to each other, or a soft kiss and a gentle
hug. I hope you forgive, even if someone breaks
your heart or tears up a book or a shoe, and know
that forgiveness is better than staying mad.
I hope you live in every moment, every sunrise,
every sunset, know that the world will tell you
that you must be everywhere all at once, but what
matters more is that you are always right here,
right now.

NEW YORK

Winter brought me to the heart of New York.
The snow falling, peppermint spice in the air.
The rush of traffic outside the hotel window—
holiday joy and anguish bundled into coats.

One morning, I went for a walk through the city,
the trees bleak against the dull gray sky. It was on
the curbside, waiting for the light to change, that a
dog brushed his nose against the edge of my coat.

His owner told me, "It is his last day today. He has
been sick for a while." I was suddenly filled
with a great sadness, and I told her so. But she replied,
"There is no need to be sad. We all know one day we
will be without our dog. But there is beauty in the
kind of honesty that is difficult and hard to swallow."

She looked down tenderly at him. "Tucker has lived.
He is living right now. We are going to enjoy the snow,
the park, his favorite spot just outside the bakery.
He loves the smell of sourdough. He has taught me
bravery and now, it is my time to be brave for him."

They went on their way, and I thought about them
for a long time afterward. Even now, years later,
every time the snow falls or I smell freshly baked
sourdough, I think fondly of that dog.
—Dear Tucker, I know you lived well.

A TALE OF THREE DOGS

This is the tale of three
very different dogs—

the first, a city dog, having
only ever lived inside an apartment,
with the occasional glimpse
of a sunrise through the skyscrapers
rising into the clouds so high,
and endless trips to cafés,
sitting under tables, waiting for crumbs
and watching the world go by.

The second, a family dog living
in the suburbs, three children to
play with in the front yard,
and morning runs, and swimming
in a big pool, many stand-offs
with the cat and even more
car trips to football games.

The third, a country dog working the land.
Dutiful and obedient, a job always to be done.
Wide-open skies and a barn to sleep in,
and occasionally a field filled with
butterflies to run through,
to the sound of the wind.

And for what it's worth, despite
coming from three different worlds,
there is one thing they share in common—
for every night, just before bed,
their humans bend down and give them
a scratch behind the ears and a long pet
on the head. "Good dog," they say,
and their eyes twinkle
as they wish good dreams
for the sleep ahead.

And while life may be a little different
everywhere you look
and all the places that you go,
an act of love is still an act of love,
no matter the size or the path it took.

CODY (WITH THE STAR ON HIS CHEST)

My in-laws had a senior Rhodesian Ridgeback called Cody, otherwise known as Cody with the Star on His Chest. You see, he was born with a patch of fur right in the middle of his chest, shaped in five points, just like a star in the sky. Cody tended to put the stars in the sky whenever he was around. He was a placid sort of dog, spending days out on the balcony in the sun, searching for morsels on the floor and as many head scratches as he could swindle. But Cody loved to walk; he could walk for miles and miles. Every day he would walk, and he would stop to smell every shrub, look up at the pinks and blues of an early morning sky, and greet the other dogs and people along the way.

In the later years, as he became older, grayer around the snout and ears, his back legs found it hard to keep up with all the walking he wanted to do. My in-laws also had another dog, Indiana, filled with young life, who could run like the wind. And even if Indiana was much faster and more energetic, Cody would still meet her by the front door, waiting for the walks he loved with my mother-in-law.

Cody was never afraid to continue doing the thing he loved most in the world.

As though he was trying to tell us that age would never define a person, that the wonder in our hearts and our desire to do the things we love don't ever cease to exist. We are no less important or curious or playful the older we become.

Although perhaps we become a little wiser, for in Cody's case, he knew if he found a nice patch of grass and sat down long enough, someone would always carry him home.

ARE YOU HOME YET?

There was an entire lifetime
between hello and goodbye.
So many beautiful memories,
now forever etched into the skyline.

When we first met, you were this tiny thing of fluff,
always wanting to play or nap or eat or have a toilet break.
And each day I was at work, I would count down the hours
to return to you. Always picturing you by the door—

Are you home yet?

Years went on, and so did the long walks together,
and games of fetch. All those vacations to the mountains;
you would always know when the trip was near, and you
would sit in your favorite chair, facing the
front yard, waiting for me—

Are you home yet?

Then I met her, and you liked her right away, always pushing
yourself into her lap, pressing your nose to hers as if you had
found another favorite person to love, so every day evolved into—

Are you both home yet?

And then a little later the baby came, and you lay by his crib
day and night. Until in the blink of an eye he was up and about.
Still, you followed him around the house as he explored.
While I worked, I wished I could have been there to see every minute,
every second and every hour, but I knew you were there to watch
it all, and still I imagined you looking from him to the door.

Are you home yet?

On that final day, when the end of your journey neared,
I kept a smile on the whole day, doing all the things you loved.
But when you weren't looking, I shed more tears
than I thought I had. How could I be ready for one last hug?

The moment I knew you were gone, I stared out the
big bay window, the warmth of the sun streaming in,
and to the bright and wide-open sky, I whispered,

"Are you home yet?"

TWO MIDDLE NAMES

On the beach one day,
I stood alone,
watching my dog as she
dug up sand and pointed
her nose
in all sorts of directions.

Until eventually, another dog
wandered up beside her
and began
to assist her in all the digging.

A mere moment later, I met
the dog's mother, and we stood for
a short while, watching as our dogs
became friends in the sand.

The dog's mother went on to say
what a lovely day for the beach,
and how impressed she was
with all of my dog's digging.
I simply smiled; she was indeed
very good at digging.
"What's her name?" she asked.
"Dakota," I replied. "And yours?"
"Simon," she said.

And she bounced on her toes,
a question lingering.
"Just Dakota?"
"Dakota Lilah," I corrected myself.
"Just Simon?"
"Actually," she replied, "his full name is
Simon James Parker Smith."
"A good name," I said, and
Simon James Parker Smith's mother beamed.

It was that day, right there on the beach
as the wind kicked up the sand and
two dogs ran and ran,
I understood that perhaps all dogs
should have middle names.

Sometimes even two.

RUFUS

One early evening as I sat curled on the sofa,
a tea with two sugars in hand and my favorite book,
fire burning and toes warm in socks and loafers,
it occurred to me my dog Rufus was awfully quiet.

And it is often in these moments certain chaos ensues—
like chewing cables or some other electrical fuse,
or diving into wastepaper baskets and eating my discarded
fake eyelashes or running off with my reading glasses.

At the thought of such chaos, I immediately rose,
calling out, "Rufus!" But naturally he did not show.
After a moment more, there was a loud crash from outside,
and I ran to see what it could be, flicking on the porch light.
The crime scene erupted before me. My flower beds had met
an unfortunate fate; gone were the petunias and the tomatoes,
upended were the trash cans, like a waste-fueled tornado.

Most noticeable in the mess that had once been my garden
was a remaining (although picked clean) chicken carcass.
And in the middle of all the complete and utter fuss
was the culprit, my dear old Scottish Terrier, Sir Rufus.
Clapping two hands together sternly and fittingly loud,
"Rufus!" I yelled. "Look at this mess—I am beyond mad!"

Sitting there rather perplexed, not moving a muscle,
Rufus stared up at me, innocent, until a sudden rustle—
the beady face of a raccoon shot up over the garbage can,
and then up onto the tree, disappearing in a single flash.

Rufus looked at me solemnly.
Why do you always blame everything on me? This is not my doing, you see.
I sighed a deep sigh, scratching my head. "Because it is
not unlike you to steal a chicken carcass or two."

I called him over. "I am sorry," I said, "for blaming you."
And with those big eyes Rufus replied, *I forgive you.*
But as I leaned in for an apologetic embrace, I spotted the
remnants of chicken stuffing all around his little face.

And Rufus, as Rufus seems to do repeatedly,
let out a small hiccup and grinned sheepishly.

THE SECRET TO LIVING

W E'D BEEN IN LOVE FOR WHAT SEEMED LIKE FOREVER, and one day late in the spring we decided to get a dog together. We searched and searched until we found her at the shelter, a rescue dog with one ear up and one ear down. The day we brought her home, our worlds were changed, turned all the way around. One particular day, distracted by life, you poured too much detergent in the washing machine. I remember hearing your squeal as the suds began to spill out and all over the floor. And the dog, she ran with me to the laundry too, and we both went sprawling across a slippery slope, right into you.

As we sat, laughing and ankle-deep in soap suds with the dog nipping at all the bubbles, I looked at you, drunk on the way you looked, enamored in the way I felt.

"What is the secret to living?" I remember asking.

And you looked back at me, and then to the dog and the mess all over the floor.

"The years will often be like one ear up and one ear down, always chasing a sunset brighter than the day before, laughing so hard you can't think straight anymore. It's about loving, forgiving, dreaming, and wishing. But most of all, it's about you, me, and the dog. That's the secret to living."

THE INTERRUPTION

On our anniversary, my love
and I had dinner by candlelight
and two glasses of wine—
before agreeing to watch our
favorite movie late into the night.

Into bed we climbed, covers warm,
pillows propped and legs entwined.
I told my love how lucky I was
for all the years our hearts had aligned.

We leaned in to whisper love with a kiss,
and our little dog, at the end of the bed,
promptly decided to push in between
as if to say, in a little dog way, *There
is no need for your affections tonight,
for all your attention should be on me.*

"Do you think she does this on purpose?"
my love said to me. For this was not the
first time our little dog had interrupted a kiss.
In fact, I was beginning to think our little dog
was determined to prevent our evening bliss.
"Of course not," I replied, and leaned in
for a kiss once more.

But there was our little dog,
steadfast and unwavering, refusing
to budge or to kindly relocate to the floor.

And then our little dog looked up at me,
squarely in the eyes, saying to me
with all her little-dog vigor and might,
Now, now, there will be none of that tonight.

FALL

The leaves have once again changed color,
    deep red and orange, enchanting and gold.
The trees stand tall in our yard, their trunks old and wise,
    having stood the test of time with stories far and wide.

And our dog Misty surely adores this time of year.
    A time to watch the leaves float down to the earth
    and wait patiently for every pile to grow bigger,
and until such time arises, to spend bounding back and forth.

With excitement, she steps outside, and I look on
    as she bounds and leaps into every pile with flair,
    and the leaves, they stick like Velcro to her long hair.

Filled with joy from all the leaping I suppose,
    she returns inside for a repose.
And as I look down at her, grinning from ear to ear,
how can I possibly not be in love with the fall—
despite all the leaves Misty brings through the door.

TOMORROW

There was a small boy, Henry,
who lived at the end of our street,
and each and every day, he would
ride the bus to and from school.

As the bus would approach the corner,
his dog, Milo, would appear on the
front porch, tail wagging, waiting.

Then Henry would step from the bus,
and Milo's tail would wag a little faster.

Milo would rush down to the end of
the driveway and greet Henry excitedly.
And Henry would greet Milo back
with just as much enthusiasm.

If ever there is a day that fills my
heart with sorrow,
     I think of Henry and his
friendship with Milo.
How they are bonded through innocence
and sincerity—
     such pure love and joy
gives me hope for tomorrow.

THE TRUTH IS IN THE STICK

A short stroll from my house,
there was a lake under the bypass.
And people would bring their dogs
to walk and to play and to splash about.

One such day, as my dog ran the length
of the sandbank with others, I happened
to meet a woman called Mary standing
on the lakeshore, one hand shielding
her eyes from the sun as she looked out
into the lake, focused on a dog swimming
back to her, balancing a stick between its teeth.
His name, I learned, was Rover.

And so, as Rover approached, Mary took
the stick and threw it back into the lake again,
and Rover dove into the water, paddling
out to the center before disappearing
under the surface for a moment or two.

As he approached again, he had a bigger stick.

Mary and Rover repeated this game over and
over again, and each time, Rover would bring
back an even bigger stick.

The final stick, more of a branch, Rover dropped
at Mary's feet, and himself too, for a small reprieve.
Mary looked at me with a smile. "Well," she said,
looking down at the smallest stick to the largest,
"I suppose every goal starts out small."

A LADY (WITH NO TEETH)

Growing up, we had a Shetland Sheepdog called Lady.
At first my father didn't want a puppy. He refused to
get one. He said there was no time for a puppy.
So, I begged my mother instead. And we ended up
with Lady, a little sheepdog from across the pond.
My father was furious. He disliked Lady before she
even arrived. He spent weeks complaining, and then
when she did arrive, he spent weeks complaining even more.
Until slowly, over time, something changed. Suddenly Lady
was always seated by Father on the couch. She was always
sitting at his heel in the kitchen, and across his lap when
he worked in his office. Always watching him as he worked
in the garden. When Lady got to her senior days, all her
teeth went missing. It was my father who sat with her night
after night and hand-fed her. He would stroke her head,
tell her she was doing the best she could. I thought back to
when my father hadn't even wanted her, then to what she became
to him, a shadow; there was nowhere my father could go
where Lady was not by his side. Perhaps this is what happens
in life. The things we do not want and the paths we never
intended to take end up being the things we need most.

THE DOOR

The door, a portal to the outside—
tall grass to run through, flowers to smell,
clouds to watch, bright sun to squint into.

Always when there is a knock, my dog
leaps from her resting spot to greet the visitor,
a lopsided grin stretched across her face.

So, too, the same smile is there every time
I walk back through the door, no matter if
if it's minutes or hours that I've been gone.

And I imagine she is saying, *You think you*
have all this time. That the people you love
will always walk back through the door.

So now, I know every tail wag means so much
more. It means every opportunity to say *I love you,*
I am so happy you walked through the door.

THE NEIGHBOR (CALLED COOPER)

NEXT DOOR TO THE VERY FIRST HOUSE I LIVED IN, THERE was a golden retriever. His name was Cooper. Cooper liked his belly rubbed. Constantly. Which was no problem for me; I liked Cooper. The second-to-last wooden paling in the neighbor's fence wasn't secured, and so Cooper would find it in himself to wiggle under the paling and trot down the driveway, making his way to most of the neighbor houses and demanding belly rubs. Of course, most obliged. And soon, Cooper was arriving on the doorstep of all the neighbors on the block: *A belly rub from you, and you*, and so on and so forth. Until it became the talk of the neighborhood.

"Why, Cooper stops me as I am unpacking my groceries," Mrs. Wilks at number forty-five would say, "but I don't mind—he is always sure to thank me!"

"Sometimes I will check the mail five times a day," Mr. Anderson at number forty-two would say, "just in case Cooper needs some love!"

One afternoon, I was sitting under my favorite tree, and it had been a particularly difficult day as days sometimes can be. Cooper trotted into the yard, tail wagging, and sat down beside me. Cooper, of course, demanded a belly rub.

"Oh, Cooper," I said, "not today."

But Cooper rolled over, and with all four paws in the air, he stared longingly up at me.

Go on, he willed with his big chestnut eyes.

Well, Cooper got his belly rub, and in return my day wasn't so difficult after all. I found my smile again in Cooper's silly face and golden fur.

I have thought about Cooper many times over the years, and what he was trying to tell me. That perhaps in life, it brings more joy to give. Even when you don't feel like giving, even when it feels much easier to take. Real success comes from all the ways I have given, like kindness and my time and compassion and in Cooper's case, all the belly rubs.

YELLOW DANDELION

Stretched all around the fields, little yellow dandelions,
holding on to each other in the changing gusts of wind.
I stand before a sea of golden petals as they sway and bend,
and I ask them how I will ever cope without my dearest friend.

And they call back to me, a glimmer of hope ready to set sail
across a sky's ocean, deep longing breaths, permission to exhale.
With a whisper of knowledge that only the dandelions know:
Sometimes strength lies in our grace to surrender and let go.

This open field where I imagine you to be, curled up under
your favorite pine tree, singing a song for all the dandelions.
With every season, your petals dance through the sky, living
on through the wind, soaring and flying in clouds so high.

So, I will not cry for this deep absence you have left.
I will remember fondly the memories just beyond the horizon.
For you will be my heart and soul for all my life,
my dearest friend; be now with the yellow dandelions.

ON BELONGING

In the late summer, the passionfruit vine
begins to bear fruit, sweet and delicious

—the splendor of regrowing and renewing
always beautiful, always bringing new hope—

I look for new beginnings in all the rays of light
surrounding the patio, where the dog and I sit

And I ask—
How do you start again, when the folds do not bend,
where do you place your love if you feel you don't fit in

And I tell him the story, all about my breaking heart,
how the long years have made many bruises and scars

With legs outstretched across the wooden pales
and a deep sigh from within, the dog exhales

In a language that speaks with poignant eyes
and in the limber way a dog can be, he says—
Surely you know, you've always belonged with me

THE LITTLE BEAGLE (WITH THE BLUE COLLAR)

THE LITTLE BEAGLE DOG, WHO HAD A BLUE COLLAR, PADDED down the road, tail high in the air, sniffing out the smells of the butcher on the corner. Before his owner woke, he had slipped under the fence to visit his butcher friend, who would surely give him some steaks. As he crossed the street in front of the florist, he saw the line of people waiting for the bus, and nobody looked particularly happy on this nice day, so the little beagle dog thought he might stop before carrying on his way.

Hello, said the little beagle dog to the elder woman in brown loafers and the young boy with a bag full of books.

How do you do? said the little beagle dog to the businesswoman in glasses and the businessman in trousers.

And on he went to greet the carpenter and the window cleaner, the lawyer and the barista. The mother and the father, and the grandmother eating a pear, the actor and the singer, and the young woman in the wheelchair.

The bus line no longer seemed so grim, for soon upon everyone's face, a smile appeared instead, and each hand reached out to pat his little head.

And after all the passengers were seen to, the little beagle dog continued on his way.

For no matter the person or what they do and say, a person always deserves some kindness to start their day.

JOY

How beautiful it is to find joy
in such simple things.
Like a huge branch, a warm blanket,
a pile of leaves or deep pools of mud,
running, and chewing on sleeves.

Through each and every day,
I have someone who asks
for nothing in return
other than to walk beside me
through every step and turn.

MY OLDEST FRIEND

My oldest friend has never asked me
why I was crying, or why I was angry,
or why on some days I just could not
bring myself to get out of bed.

My oldest friend has never judged me
for the mistakes I have made in my life,
or turned away when I have needed someone.

My oldest friend has lain down beside me
for hours on end, only ever moving to place
a head on my chest.

My oldest friend, with a wet nose in my face
or a paw on my shoulder or eyes that seem to
see right to my very soul, has without ever saying
a single word, promised me, *I'm always right here.*

HERO IS HIS NAME

My dog, his name is Hero.
I found him with other puppies
like him,
little eager things, wanting food.

Off went the puppies toward the call,
not Hero though, he waited,
greeting me at the door—
and so, I decided,
"Well now, I can't leave,
not without you."

And time happened, be not still,
so Hero grew, and grew—
and grew.
Taller than I expected,
taller than me, (probably)
taller than you.

But I've never felt safer
than in the moments
he considered (with certainty)
that I was in danger.

How he would leap
between
me and the suspicious
stranger.
Or sometimes it was
the vacuum;
how dare it rumble
toward me?

A toothy growl,
so low:
Be gone, you monstrous thing.
Be gone.

And sometimes
(or more often than sometimes)
it would be me
protecting him:

thunder as it clashed—
rain as it fell,
lightning as it struck,
those loud alarms
blaring from the fire truck.

And like that first day,
he still waits by the door
with those big brown eyes
I adore, adore.

For as long as the earth
upon which we walk
continues to be,
my best friend he is,
forever and always—
my Hero and me.

THERE YOU ARE

There you are with your pointy little ears;
I remember the day we brought you home
like it was just yesterday,
the memories we've made since then—
like all the nights teaching you to sit or stay,
you stealing socks and running down the hallway.

There you are with your tiny little paws,
always rummaging through shopping bags,
searching for one more snack or treat.
Always ready to be a bright light
and a friend to all the people you meet.

There you are with your wet little nose.
How you have brought me relief in times
of struggle, when the world is sad and dark.
How we now find joy in the little things
like the beach, the woods, and the park.

There you are with the sweetest little heart,
up and ready to go about your day,
always showing such humility
in all the things you set out to do.
Of course, I'll love you for infinity.

THE BABY BIRD

One August evening, under the pink and lilac sky,
our Alsatian found a small blue jay beneath our
honeysuckle tree, squawking and carrying on,
for two crows circled above, much bigger than
the baby blue jay. And so gently, our dog lifted the
baby bird into his mouth and carried it over
to our porch, out of harm's way. The blue jay, having
made all sorts of noises under the tree, now remained
unperturbed, watching, I suspect, for our dog's next move.
After a thought, our dog went back to those crows still circling
in the sky, and he barked until they flew off in a frenzy.
While a bark is just a bark to many, I am quite sure he said,
Hey there, crow, pick on someone your own size, you know!

MOMENTS

There are moments when the thoughts
        are never ending,
when the world feels as though
        it is moving faster
than the beating of your heart.

And you begin to lose yourself
        in the mess and motions.
Suddenly you forget the little things,
        and the world shrivels,
becoming nothing more than a dark shadow.

But in the midst of the madness,
        I look to my dog.

I watch as he stops to inspect every small
        blade of grass
and blinks up into the sky, how he stands still to watch
        the birds fly by.

Perhaps this is how life should be led,
        stopping to smell the grass,
admiring the sky,
living in every moment
        before it passes us by.

KISSING THE BEES

We were on the front porch.
You had rolled over and decided
you wanted to kiss the bees
in the early morning.

I was nervous, having seen what bee stings
can do to a dog's nose. But you went over and
greeted them anyway.

And I watched you as you padded all
around the yard.
Nothing really fazed you.
No problem too big to handle.

And I wanted to live my life like that,
showing courage and love to even the things
that might hurt us.

I wanted to live like a gentle rustle
in the morning leaves.
I wanted my life to be as simple
as kissing the bees.

THE LONG WALK HOME

Life continues on. Through the winter months
and into the spring, it goes on. And through life
there will always be one particular story that stays
with you. Even after years of forgotten happenings
and chaotic days filled with more and more memories,
there will always be one story that just simply sticks.
For me, it's the long walk home.

It was late in the fall. The pumpkin harvest had begun,
and the trees had started to shake their leaves, bright
orange, yellow, and red filling the woods that surrounded
the little house in which I lived.

One day, after a week of rain, I was eager to move about,
so I called on my dogs and went out into the woods, a
beautiful morning when the sun was still high up on the hill.
We had walked the same path one hundred times or more,
having many conversations throughout the years.

After a while, I thought to myself that the walk was
becoming rather long. Normally it would not take
as many steps to get back to the house. What's more, all
the trees began to look the same, repeating over
and over again the same lines and patterns.

And I looked down at both my dogs and said,
"Perhaps we are lost."
But they didn't seem to think so.

So onward we pressed, moving through the tall grass,
stopping occasionally to smell a wildflower or two,
watch a bird fly from one tree to the other, marvel at
the marigold and how beautiful it will grow. Just me
following my feet and my dogs following their nose.

And suddenly, above the hill, we saw our little house
with the thatched roof and roses growing in the garden.
"Good dogs," I mused. "You've found the way home."
And off they went, tails in the air, noses to the ground,
for home is where the heart is and can always be found.

And if I could leave you with any advice in this
wide-open world, it would be this—
today and tomorrow and in all the things you do,
give your dog a scratch behind the ears and remind them,
"Life is so much brighter when I am with you."

To all the dogs that were, are, and will be—
you are all good, every single one.

ACKNOWLEDGMENTS

Firstly, thank you to Michelle for taking a chance on this book and supporting the idea from the first moment it was brought to you. There is no better home for it than Central Avenue and it has been a joy to work with you through this process. To Jessica, thank you for all your edits and for making the entire process seamless and enjoyable.

To my team, for all your hard work always. To Justin, my brilliant artist—it is an honor to work with you. Thank you for creating some truly amazing pieces, especially of Hero and Dakota!

To my family and friends—a book is never possible without you!

To my readers, those of you who have been on this journey from the beginning or joined recently or perhaps with this very book, thank you for your support. I hope that you can share these poems with your four-legged friends. If you would like to write to me, you can contact me on courtney@pepperbooks.org. Your thoughts and stories are always welcome, and so, too, are pictures of your dogs!

Hero, Courtney & Dakota

Courtney Peppernell is a best-selling author from Sydney, Australia, best known for her *Pillow Thoughts* poetry collection. The series has achieved acclaimed success worldwide, with more than a million copies sold. Courtney spends her days writing and working on many projects with her beloved dogs in tow. She hopes to continue exploring expression and the art of healing through stories, novels, and poetry for years to come.

Instagram: @courtneypeppernell
Twitter: @CourtPeppernell
TikTok: @courtneypeppernell
Pillow Thoughts App out now

Dear Reader,

You are holding an edition designed exclusively for Target stores. On the following pages are two very special pieces: one for my dog Hero and the other for my dog Dakota.

I hope you find the same love and support in those that surround you as I find in these two.

All my love,

Courtney xx

MY LITTLE DOG

The light is soft through the window,
      the day rising.
So, too, my little dog. With a long stretch
      and a mopish yawn,
her head appears, a familiar sight each morning,
much like the grass always dressed in dew.
She checks to see if I have awoken too.

Only for a moment, I am gone out the door
to retrieve the mail and a coffee, and when I return,
my little dog greets me in abounding delight
as though I have been gone an entire season—
and how could I not adore
      the simplicity and wonder
of being another soul's entire reason?

I look for the words to describe the joy
of watching a little dog be a little dog—
darting this way and darting that way,
chasing dandelions floating through the air.
Long, drawn-out days by the beach,
      dancing
through salt and foamy sea spray.

There have been many days where my little dog
        was the truest friend I had—
and in these frailer moments, my little dog
        saved my thoughts
from being too dark and my feelings too sad.

Our favorite time of year, when life awakens
from the slumberous winter to the crisp joyfulness
of springtime and we walk the fields of lavender,
my little dog bounding ahead in playfulness,
        we pause
to smell the sweet honey pollen in the atmosphere.

There is no greater lesson that has been taught
than to simply relish a moment: rising early,
a long walk, a day that is yours, a future of purpose.
        My little dog teaches me so,
in all her little-dog earnest.

In the sun-soaked afternoons, we lie out on the porch
watching clouds drift by and bees dip between petals.
There is such happiness in the stillness of time.
        And so, we wait
for the first signs of stars and for the night to settle.

Often I have wondered, if the whole world carried
the same forgiveness and kindness that exists
      in the wag of a tail, the spring in a step,
and eyes that look deep down into the pockets of a
      soul—
then surely this world in which you and I exist
would be brighter, living with more meaning and truth,
      a gift.

My little dog is the light forever beating within my
      heart.
My sweetest friend holds the most precious part
in my story—every line, chapter, and epilogue.
So, always I ask,
      where would I be without my little dog?

A HERO'S JOURNEY

THE DAY IS BRIGHT, THE SKY SOFT AND CLEAR. IT RAINED all week, only for the sun to return in hopeful bursts of light on the very last Sunday of the month. We walk, my dog Hero and I, along the backroads, toward the edge of the woods. He keeps his nose to the ground, following the overgrown grass all the way to the entrance of the trail. It will take us deep into the forest, where the thickest trees have lived for centuries. I crouch down beside Hero and he looks at me, brown eyes glistening in the sunlight.

"Are you ready?" I ask as I unclip the leash.

He strides ahead as if to say yes.

All around us, white clovers are scattered in the soil, the first signs of the season changing once more.

We are swallowed by the forest.

The air is crisp and I breathe it in, the sweet scent of pollen filling my lungs. The earth is soft beneath us, damp and muddy from the rain. We pause briefly, and Hero inspects the wooden signpost pointing us further into the trail. Wildflower shoots grow all around the base, and he is intrigued by them. I wonder how many others have stopped in this very spot. If they, too, noticed the wildflowers beginning to grow once more. If they, too, noticed the tiny spots of color returning to the forest, the darkness retreating and making way for the light.

"I thought it would rain forever," I say, and Hero looks up at me earnestly.

The storm never lasts, he says.

We move past the signpost, treading over broken branches, our steps echoing into the canopy above us. There is a bird calling from somewhere in the trees overhead. The sound fills the gaps between the leaves. A call is returned, and then another, a song reverberating all around us. Hero stops and looks up, listening.

"Are you coming?" I say, passing him.

Stop for a moment, he replies. *Listen.*

"I've heard them before."

It's always good to just listen.

I walk back to him, glancing up into the canopy, and we listen to the song together. I have not heard these calls before, and they sound different, a sharp, shrill whistle. I tell Hero this.

"It sounds different today," I say.

Hero nods knowingly and walks ahead.

Every day is different if you listen, he says.

Soon we come to a park bench, foliage wrapped around the base of its weathered legs. Beside it, a fading plaque. A fresh red orchid has been gently placed beside it. I read the inscription: *For Scout, thank you for your service.* Underneath, a set of pawprints is carved into the stone. We stay for a moment, and I think of Scout and of the someone who brought the red orchid.

There are many braver than me, Hero says.

"Me too," I reply.

He sits down beside me. *Some dogs do extraordinary things, like military dogs and police dogs, or three-legged survivor dogs, some with stories you can't quite believe.*

I look down at him curiously. "Yes, I suppose that's true."

Do you mind that I am none of these things? he asks. *That I am just a dog?*

I smile. "You are my dog," I say.

We leave the plaque and the red orchid behind.

Deeper into the forest, we find a waterfall. The water rushes down the side of the rock face in a way that makes us admire how it pools into the stream below; specks of sunlight collide and create bursts of color. It is a dreamlike view—and there is magic in dreaming. I think of Hero asleep at the foot of my bed each evening, his snout twitching, paws softly tapping the floorboards beneath his mat.

"What do you dream of, when you dream?" I ask.

I am often running, Hero says. *And also eating*, he adds.

"Am I in any of them?" I ask.

All of them, Hero replies.

We follow the stream as it leads to the creek, a bubbling current risen from the rain. The water pools around moss-stained rocks, the fallen tree leaves floating away with the current.

"Be careful," I say to Hero, but he shows no fear; he walks freely over rocks and moss, broken twigs and branches.

"Don't fall," I warn, but Hero is far more interested in the small tadpoles darting beneath the water's surface, his tail thumping the air. Suddenly he paws at the water. It splashes and sprays upward. He barks, and it rings out through the forest.

He looks at me, eager and excited. *Go on*, he says.

"I feel silly," I reply.

Go on, he repeats, eyes bright, smiling.

I yield, and I stomp my foot into the water, then again, until we are both splashing about. Hero is barking and I am laughing. How simple yet infectious a dog's joy is. I do not know what I ever did without it. My heart swells, and I splash water at Hero.

"Thank you," I say.

For what? Hero asks.

"For teaching me joy."

We find a place to sit on the embankment, the sunlight streaming through gaps in the canopy, a spotlight amid the dense forest. It is warm against my skin. Time feels as though it is passing more slowly, and the trees creak as if discussing the day. I notice a tree stump across the embankment, wondering what happened to it.

"I wonder who broke it?" I ask Hero, and he notices the tree stump too.

That's not so much the point, he says.

"Not to break?"

It broke, but it survived, he says.

"There is foliage regrowing," I observe. "Perhaps it will heal."

It will take time, Hero says, *like most things.*

He stretches lazily, enjoying the sun and the sounds of the brook babbling.

My phone vibrates in my pocket, and as I retrieve it, I instinctively open my emails. A dozen have flooded my inbox.

Be here, Hero says, noticing my phone.

"There are just some things I need to do."

You can always do them, he says. *You can't always be in this moment with me.*

I look to him and realize he is right.

"Okay," I say, and I stretch my legs out alongside his.

We leave the embankment, and the trail narrows. The sunlight disappears briefly, and we tread more carefully over the understory of the forest, the thickets of shrub and evergreen clumping together in unison. It is not long before we find a nest, fallen from a tree hollow. Hero meanders over to it, and inside a baby bird huddles. It squawks as it notices Hero, fearful.

"It probably thinks it's your lunch," I say.

Hero picks it up gently and places it back into the hollow of the trunk, where it is safe and free from the dangers of the forest floor.

Kindness is always more nourishing, he says.

We carry on walking the trail as it twists and bends, until we are stopped by a tree that has fallen across the path, its thick trunk uprooted from the soil that held it steady and thriving for so long. I study it for a moment, wondering how to climb over it. Hero looks at me, and it is a weary look, for he cannot jump so high nor climb so far anymore. When he was young, we would climb and leap and run together. He would revel in his search for wild rabbits, running and exploring the fields. But with age, like all things, our bodies slow. I hold out my hand, and he nuzzles his graying snout underneath it.

"Old boy," I whisper.

Perhaps we can go around, he says, hopeful.

"No," I muse, "that will take us all day."

I lean down and gather him into my arms.

When did you become so strong? he asks.

"When you started carrying me all those years ago," I reply.

We climb over the fallen tree.

The day is changing, cooling. The sun darts between the trees, sinking with each passing minute. Hero stops a moment, checks that I am still following behind.

"I'm still here," I say.

Suddenly, a movement diverts his attention, and he dashes after the noise, disappearing into the shrubbery. I hurry after him, calling for him. For a few bleak moments, I cannot see, hear, or find him, and my heart sits caught between my throat and my lungs.

"Hero!" I call, but there is no sign of him. "Hero!" I repeat, my voice louder now, but there is still no trace of him.

I find my way through low-hanging branches and weeds and emerge into a clearing. The trees are parted, there are more signposts, and I see Hero waiting by one of them. His ears soften as he sees me, and his tail wags. As I walk to him, I push down the thought that one day I will emerge into a clearing and Hero will no longer be waiting by the signpost—at least not in this world. It is perhaps the hardest truth we will know, that a dog does not live forever.

"I thought I had lost you," I say, reaching him.

He looks at me curiously. *You'll never lose me*, he replies. *I am always waiting for you.*

I place my hand on his head, scratch him behind the ears, and say, "Let's go home."

As we walk back toward home, I look for Hero in the fading sunlight between the trees, catching glimpses of him, tail wagging, nose to the ground, weaving through the tall grass. Every so often, he stops and glances back toward me. It is here I will hold him forever. It is in these precious, beautiful moments I imagine all the dogs that were, that are, and that are yet to be, will exist forever. Never too far from us, always glancing back to make sure we are right behind them.

HERO

DAKOTA